D0100161

The life cycle of a Bean

Ruth Thomson

PowerKiDS press.
New York

Property of
Welch Elementary School
2620 Leverenz Road
Naperville, IL 60564

Published in 2008 by The Rosen Publishing Group, Inc.
29 East 21st Street, New York, NY 10010

Copyright © 2008 Wayland/The Rosen Publishing Group, Inc.

All rights reserved. No part of this book may be reproduced in any form without permission from the publisher, except by a reviewer.

First Edition

Photo Credits: All cover images and 1, 4-5, 8, 9, 10, 11, 12, 13, 14, 16, 17, 20, 21, 23 Adam White/naturepl.com; 6 Geoff Dann/DK Images; 7 Roger Phillips/DK Images; 13 Oxford Scientific Films; 15 Premaphoto/naturepl.com; 18 John B. Free/naturepl.com; 19Meul/ARCO/naturepl.com; 22 wikipedia/nl:Gebruiker:Rasbak

Library of Congress Cataloging-in-Publication Data

Thomson, Ruth, 1949-
Bean / Ruth Thomson. -- 1st ed.
p. cm. -- (Learning about life cycles: The life cycle of a bean)
Includes index.
ISBN-13: 978-1-4042-3714-8 (library binding)
ISBN-10: 1-4042-3714-3 (library binding)
1. Beans--Juvenile literature. 2. Beans--Development--Juvenile literature. I. Title.
SB327.T46 2007
635'.65--dc22

2006033084

Manufactured in China

Contents

Beans grow here	4
What Is a broad bean?	6
Planting	8
Roots	10
Shoot	12
Leaves	14
Flowers	16
Pollination	18
Beans	20
New seeds	22
Bean life cycle	23
Glossary	24
Index	24
Web Sites	24

Beans grow here

Broad beans are good to eat. People grow them in their gardens or **vegetable plots**. Farmers grow thousands of broad bean plants in enormous fields.

What is a broad bean

A broad bean is a **seed**. Several grow together inside a pod. The tough, thick skin of the pod protects the beans. The beans we eat are soft and green.

This is what a bean looks like inside.

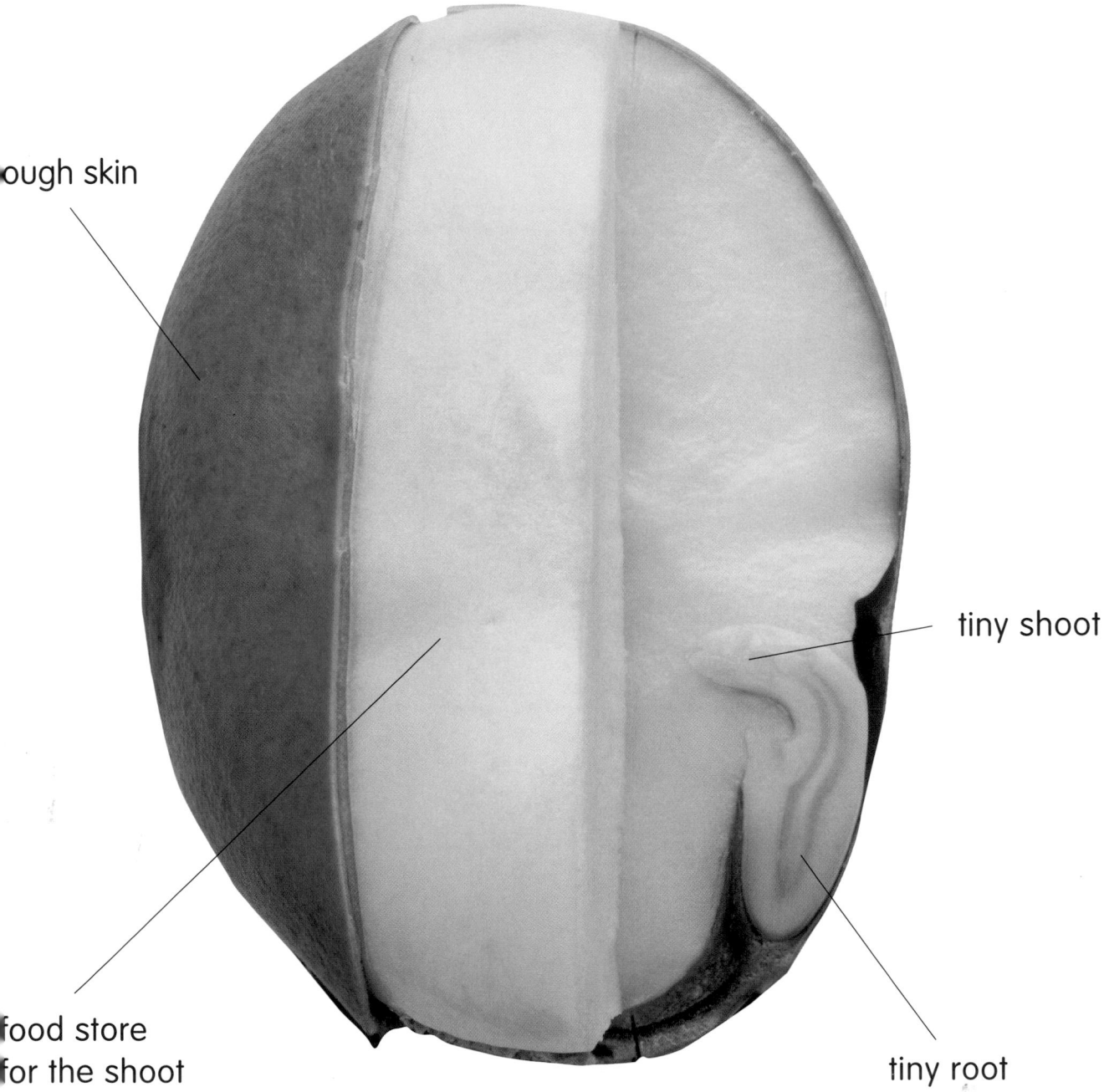

Planting

People save a store of beans as seeds for planting. They leave the beans to dry. The beans turn hard and brown.

In the springtime,
the beans are
planted in warm, damp soil.
Water makes the beans swell.

Roots

The hard skin of the bean splits.
A tiny **root** pokes out.
It starts to grow
down into
the soil.

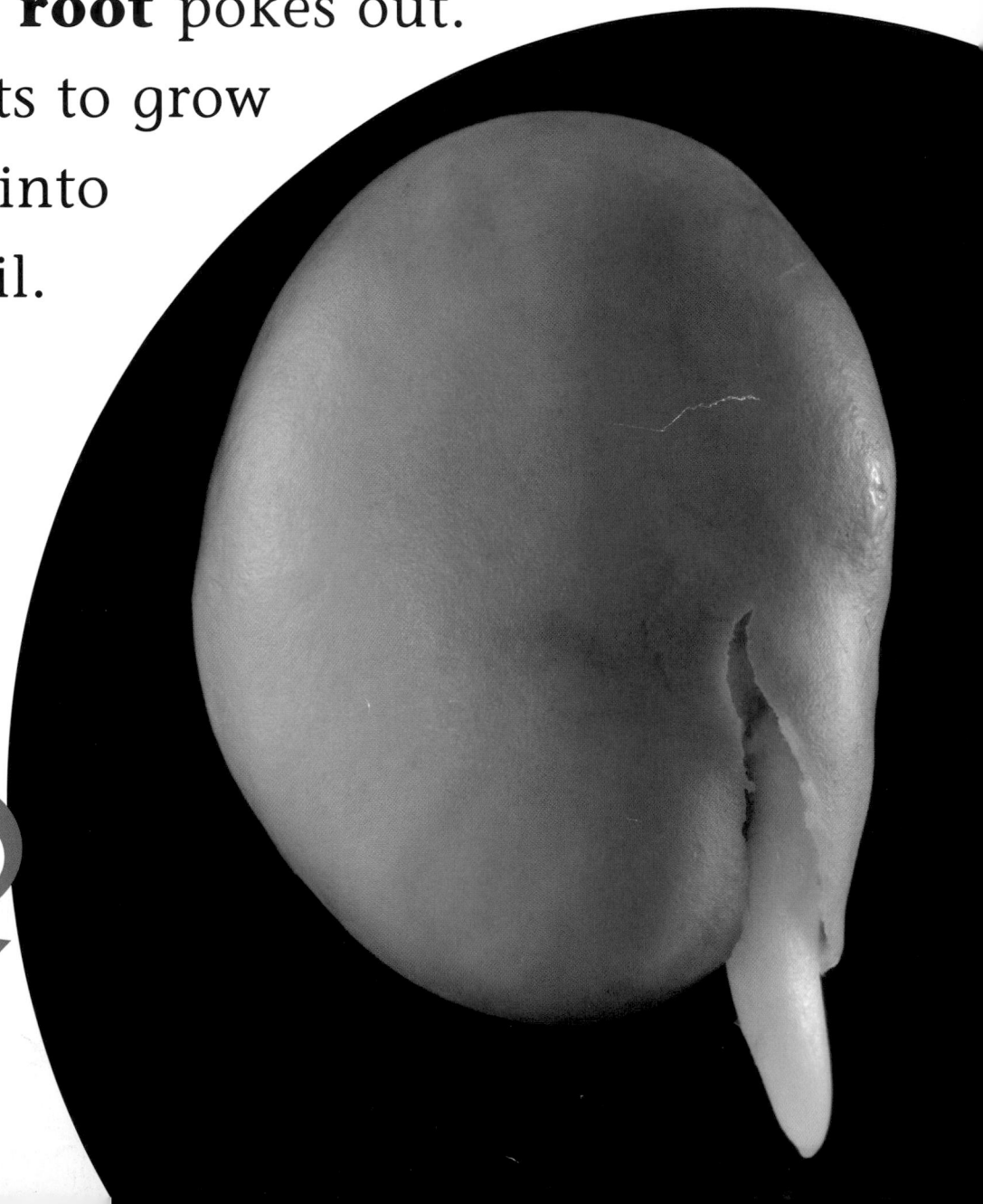

1 week

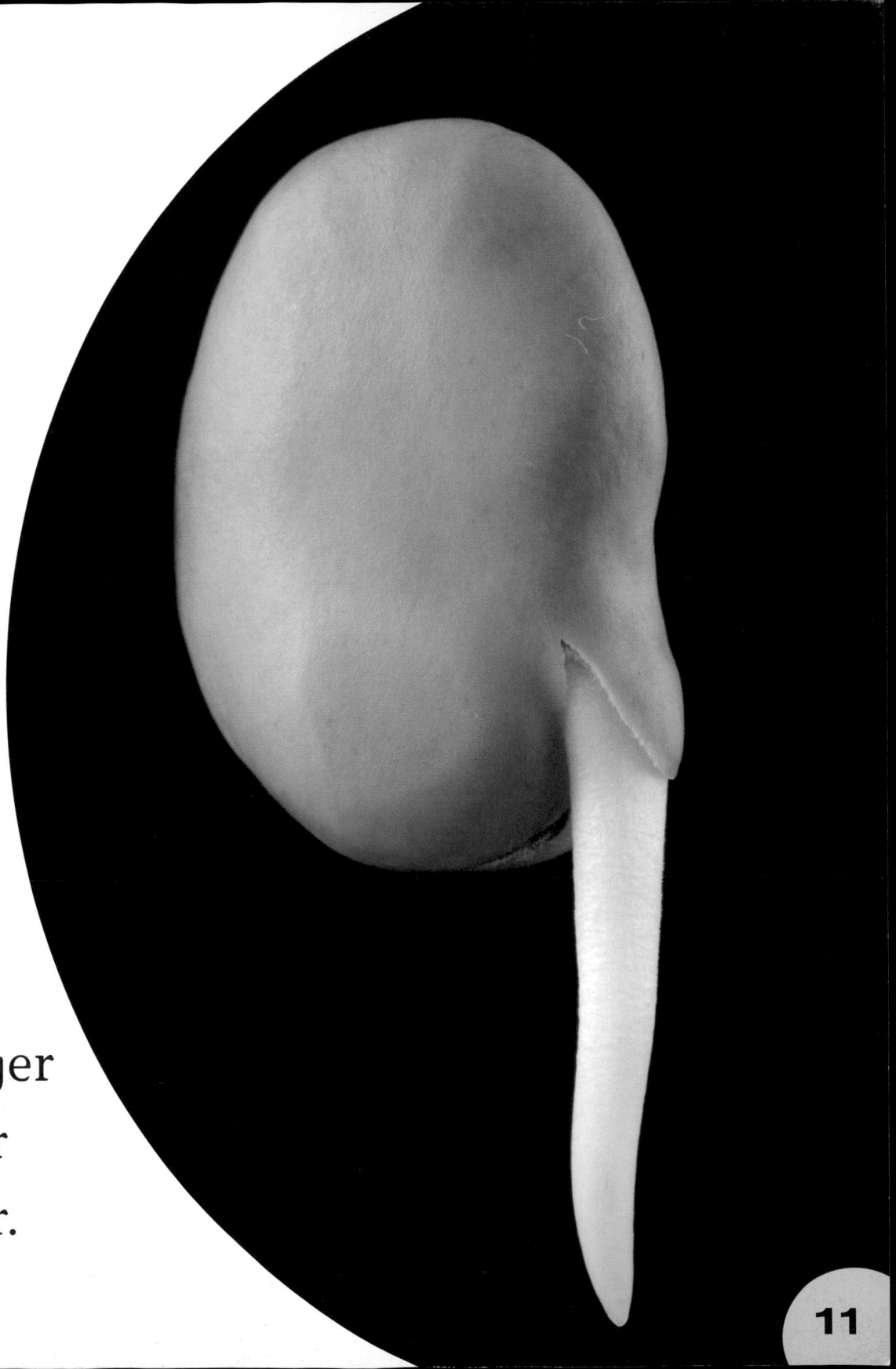

Every day,
the root
grows longer
and longer
and longer.

Shoot

A **shoot** starts to grow upward. On its tip are tiny **leaves**. These bend downward, so they do not break as the shoot pushes through the soil.

The shoot pops out of the soil. The leaves uncurl and turn darker. Side **roots** grow from the main root. Tiny hairs on them take up water from the soil.

Leaves

Now the plant has used up the bean's food store. The **leaves** spread out to catch sunlight. Leaves use water from the soil, sunlight, and air to make food.

Blackfly lay their eggs on the leaves. When the young **hatch**, they eat the leaves. Ladybugs gobble up Black flies, so the leaves do not become too damaged.

Flowers

Every week the plant grows taller and the **leaves** grow bigger. Flower **buds** begin to form.

The buds open out into white flowers. In the center of each flower are tiny grains of yellow **pollen** and a sweet liquid called **nectar**.

Pollination

Bees crawl inside the flowers to sip the **nectar** and collect the **pollen**. The black lines on the petals point the way to the nectar.

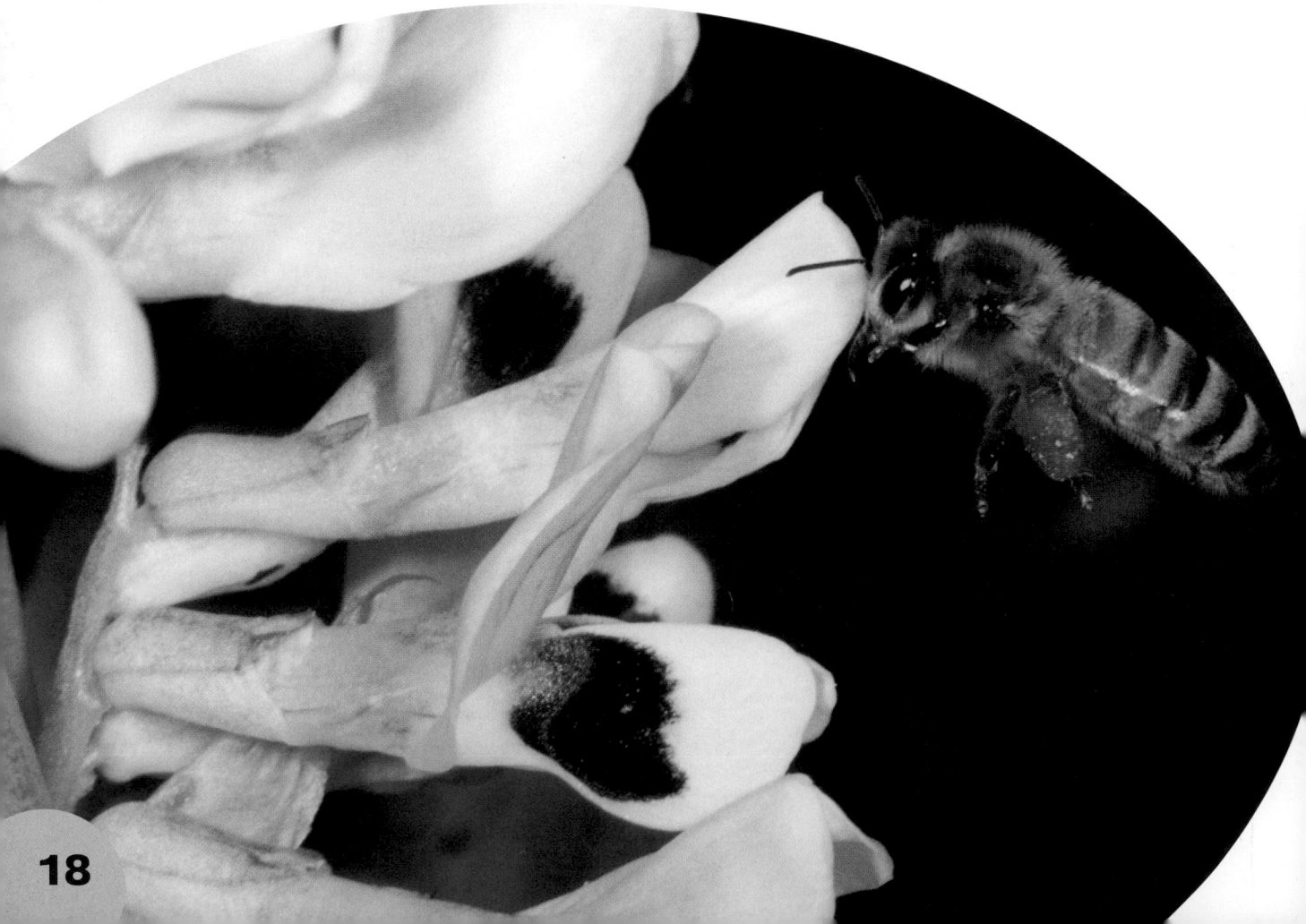

As a bee flies from one flower to another, pollen sticks to its hairy legs. Pollen from one flower rubs off onto the next one. This pollen helps to make new beans.

Beans

Now the flower is no longer needed. Its petals **wither** and fall off, leaving a pod with tiny beans inside.

The beans swell and grow. The pods become long and heavy. People pick the pods before the beans are fully grown, when they are tastiest.

New seeds

In the fall, the bean plant shrivels and dies. Unpicked pods turn brown and fall to the ground. Some beans are collected for planting next spring.

Bean life cycle

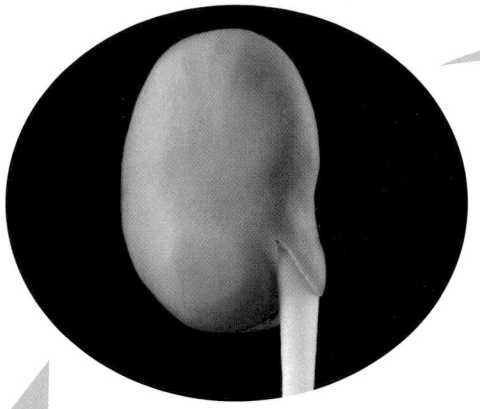

Bean
The bean is planted. After 1 week, a **root** grows.

Leaves
A **shoot** grows up out of the soil. The **leaves** uncurl.

Flowers
The plant grows taller, and after 12 weeks, flowers appear.

Bean pods
After 18 weeks, the beans are ready to be picked.

Glossary

bud a swelling on a stem that will grow into a flower or leaves

leaves the part of a plant that makes food

nectar the sweet juice inside a flower

pollen the grains of powder in the center of a flower

root the underground part of a plant that takes in water from the soil

seed the part of a plant that grows into a new plant

shoot the first leaves of a new plant

vegetable plot a small piece of land that people use for growing plants

wither to shrink and dry up

Web Sites

Due to the changing nature of Internet links, PowerKi Press has developed an online list of Web sites related to the subject of this book. This site is regula updated. Please use this link to access this list: www.powerkidslinks.com/llc/bean/

Index

bean 4, 5, 6–7, 8–9, 10, 14, 20–21, 22, 23
bees 18, 19
black flies 15
buds 16, 17

flowers 16-17, 18, 19, 20, 23
ladybugs 15
leaves 12, 13, 14-15, 16, 23

nectar 17, 18

petals 18, 20
planting 8–9
pod 6, 20, 21, 22, 23
pollen 17, 18, 19
pollination 18–19

roots 7, 10–11, 13, 23

seed 6, 8
shoot 7,12-13, 23
skin 6, 7, 10
soil 9, 10, 12, 13, 14, 23
sunlight 14

vegetable plot 4

water 9, 13, 14